MULTICULTURAL READING SERIES

BOOK • 1

by Vivienne Hodges, Ph.D.
& Stuart Margulies, Ph.D.

EDUCATIONAL DESIGN, INC.   EDI 352

ACKNOWLEDGMENTS

The authors wish to thank the following for their kind permission to reprint selections as indicated below.

"Elizabeth Eckford Goes to School" excerpt from THE LONG SHADOW OF LITTLE ROCK, by Daisy Bates. Copyright © 1962 David McKay. Reprinted by permission of Random House, Inc./Alfred A. Knopf. Inc.

"The Migrants" adapted from "The Circuit" by Francisco Jiménez, Arizona Quarterly, Autumn 1973. Copyright © 1973 Francisco Jiménez. Reprinted by permission of the author.

TABLE OF CONTENTS

INTRODUCTION

This is a book that will help you read better. It is also a book about some interesting and unusual people.

- You will read about a young Hispanic lawman named Elfego Baca. Elfego once held off a bunch of 80 wild cowboys in a gunfight that lasted two days.

- You will read about a young African-American girl named Elizabeth Eckford. Elizabeth had to face a screaming mob and soldiers with guns on her first day in high school.

- You will read about a poor, sickly Chinese man named Lue Gim Gong. He was a genius with plants. He invented a new kind of orange.

- You'll read about Jackie Robinson. Jackie was the first African-American to play baseball in the major leagues.

This book contains 20 stories. They are about Native Americans, and Americans whose ancestors came here from places as far apart as Africa and Mexico. There are also stories about people from Puerto Rico and Vietnam and Jamaica and China.

The authors of this book hope that you will enjoy reading this book about the many different kinds of people in our country and in our world.

ELFEGO BACA

COURTESY NEW MEXICO STATE RECORDS CENTER AND ARCHIVES

Elfego Baca, the fearless Hispanic sheriff of Socorro County in New Mexico. The rifle he holds is one that he took from Pancho Villa, a revolutionary general from Mexico. Villa offered a reward of $30,000 for Baca, dead or alive. Nobody dared to try and collect it.

1
TOP GUN IN NEW MEXICO

A hundred years ago, the West was famous for its gunfighters. Most were outlaws. But one of the most famous gunfighters was a Hispano lawman named Elfego Baca.

Elfego lived in Socorro, a small town in the state of New Mexico. The people of Socorro were peaceful Hispanos. Their ancestors had founded the town hundreds of years before. But on Saturday nights, Socorro became noisy and dangerous. Anglo miners and cowboys came to town. They gambled and got drunk. Some were outlaws. Most of them carried guns, and many of them got into gunfights. They used Hispano citizens for target practice. No one dared to stop them.

Elfego wanted to protect his people. His father was a lawman, and Elfego wanted to be a lawman, too. He later said, "I wanted the outlaws to hear my steps a block away from me." But even though he hated outlaws, Elfego learned how to use a gun from one of the most famous outlaws in the West—Billy the Kid. He learned well. By the age of 19, Elfego was the best shot in town.

One day, Elfego's father killed two Anglo cowboys in a fight. The cowboys had broken the law. The local judge knew Elfego's father was right, but he put Elfego's father in jail anyway. The judge was afraid of the other cowboys and of the rich and powerful ranchers who had hired them. Elfego wasn't afraid. He waited for a dark night. Then he sawed a hole in the jail wall. His father was free.

Elfego had a cousin named Pedro who was a lawman in the town of Frisco. Frisco was a dangerous town like Socorro. Pedro needed help. He sent for Elfego.

As soon as he came to Frisco, Elfego found trouble. A drunken cowboy was firing his guns at people. Elfego arrested him. This angered the other cowboys in town. They didn't want a Hispano to arrest an Anglo. A bunch of cowboys came to free their friend. One of them fired at Elfego. Elfego fired back. Then he backed into a wooden shed. It was the start of one of the West's most famous gunfights.

Eighty cowboys surrounded Elfego's shed. All night long they fired their guns. They fired more than four thousand shots. Everything inside the shed was filled with bullet holes—except Elfego. The earth floor of the shed had been dug out below the level of the ground outside. Elfego just lay flat on his belly . The cowboys' shots were all too high.

By morning, the cowboys were sure that Elfego was dead. Then they smelled food. It was Elfego cooking breakfast.

The cowboys attacked again. They tried to burn the shed and to blow it up. For 33 hours they tried to get at Elfego. Elfego's guns always stopped them. Four cowboys died and eight were wounded. Finally there was a truce.

Elfego was put on trial for killing the four cowboys. But the jury said Elfego was innocent. He had the right to protect himself when the cowboys tried to shoot him.

Elfego was a hero. He became Sheriff of Socorro County and a famous lawman. He defended the Hispano people. Criminals were terrified of him. Once he had the job of rounding up several of the county's worst criminals. Instead of going after them, he just wrote each one a letter. "If you don't give yourself up," the letter said, "I'll know that you intend to resist arrest, and I will feel justified in shooting you on sight when I come after you." The frightened criminals came to the jail and gave up without firing a shot.

But Elfego was not content to be just a gunman on the side of the law. He also studied law, and he became a lawyer. He was an excellent lawyer. He was allowed to speak before the United States Supreme Court. This was a great honor. Only a few lawyers are allowed do this. He also served as mayor and as a school superintendent.

Elfego Baca lived to be 80 years old. And he died in bed!

GLOSSARY

Anglo Someone whose ancestors are English, or whose first language is English.

Hispano Someone whose ancestors are Spanish, or someone whose first language is Spanish. In New Mexico, it usually refers to Spanish-speaking people whose ancestors settled in New Mexico several hundred years ago.

innocent Not guilty.

superintendent A supervisor; a boss.

truce An agreement in which two sides that are fighting agree to stop fighting for a while.

EXERCISES

SEQUENCE

1. Put these events in order:

    A) Elfego became the lawman of Frisco.
    B) Elfego became sheriff of Sorocco County.
    C) Elfego wrote letters to criminals.
    D) Elfego rescued his father.

CAUSE AND EFFECT

2. Eighty cowboys fired their guns at Elfego. They didn't kill him because—

    A) he was the sheriff.
    B) they were firing blanks.
    C) he was lying on the floor.
    D) he was cooking breakfast.

FACT/ OPINION

3. Which of these statements is NOT an opinion?

    A) Elfego was a hero.
    B) Elfego was the greatest sheriff of the West.
    C) Elfego led an interesting life.
    D) Elfego killed four cowboys in a gunfight.

SENTENCE COMPLETION

4. Elfego Baca wanted to protect the people living in the small towns of New Mexico. These _____ were badly treated by the cowboys.

    A) miners
    B) Anglos
    C) Hispanos
    D) sheriffs

CHARACTER'S MOTIVATION

    5. Why did cousin Pedro send for Elfego?

        A) Pedro needed help.
        B) Pedro wanted more money.
        C) The Hispanos wanted to kill Pedro.
        D) Pedro wanted Elfego's help in getting out of jail.

DRAWING CONCLUSIONS

    6. Elfego respected the law.

       Elfego was good with a gun.

       These TWO facts explain why—

        A) Elfego became a lawyer.
        B) Elfego did a good job as a lawman.
        C) Pedro quit his job.
        D) Socorro was a dangerous town.

WRITE ABOUT—

    7. Imagine that Elfego Baca is coming to speak at your school assembly. You have the honor of introducing him. What would you say? (You must say it in 5 sentences or less.)

2
NURSE ON THE BATTLEFIELD

Soldiers get injured in wars. When this happens, special soldiers called medics take them to waiting helicopters. Helicopters fly them to the hospital. Doctors are there to help them.

In the 1850's, this didn't happen. Wounded soldiers lay on the battlefield for hours. Sometimes they would cry and bleed for days. Many died. No one helped them.

One woman decided she would help. She had no money. She had no rich friends to pay her. She wasn't a doctor. But she wanted to help wounded soldiers, and she did. She was a black woman from the West Indies, and her name was Mary Seacole.

Mary was born on the island of Jamaica. Her mother ran a small hotel there. Mary helped her mother with the cooking and the hotel work, but her chief love was nursing. As a child, she nursed everything. She even took care of sick cats and dogs. She didn't know much about medicine, although she learned a little from Jamaican doctors. In those days, there were no schools for nurses. There were no drugstores either. So Mary made her own medicines.

In 1851, thousands of people in Jamaica got sick from a deadly disease called cholera. Many of them died. But Mary was able to cure others with her own special medicines. People were amazed at Mary. She was better at healing people than the doctors.

In 1854, a war began in Europe. Mary wanted to help the wounded soldiers. But the war was six thousand miles away from Jamaica. It seemed impossible for Mary to travel so far. Yet she did the impossible. First, she went to England. There, she offered to nurse the wounded soldiers. The army turned her down.

But Mary would not quit. She traveled to the war zone anyway. There she found thousands of sick and injured soldiers. Nobody was treating their wounds properly. Many of them caught diseases in the dirty hospitals. So Mary opened her own hospital. She spent all her own money on medicines and bandages. In this new hospital, Mary cooked good food. She nursed the sick and wounded. One of her patients was a nephew of the Queen of England.

Mary's bravery was amazing. She didn't wait for someone to bring wounded soldiers to her. She walked straight into the middle of the battle. She wasn't afraid of the guns. She looked for wounded soldiers and helped them with food and bandages.

There was another famous nurse who helped the soldiers in the war. Her name was Florence Nightingale. But Florence became sick herself and had to go home. Mary Seacole kept her hospital open until the very end of the war.

When the war ended Mary was poor, sick, and wounded. She had spent all her money on the soldiers. Her friends raised money for her. Many famous and wealthy people sent in money.

Mary Seacole died back home in Jamaica. Her name is not well known. But it belongs high on the list of men and women who spent their lives caring for others.

GLOSSARY

helicopters Aircraft that can fly straight up and down as well as forward. Helicopters have a large overhead propeller (called a rotor) that lets them fly this way.

wounded Injured in battle.

zone Area or region. A war zone is the place where the fighting armies are.

EXERCISES

MAIN IDEA

1. This selection is mainly about—

   A) a war in Europe
   B) why people fought
   C) a nurse who helped soldiers
   D) living in Jamaica

OPPOSITE MEANINGS

2. The author says that the army <u>turned Mary Down</u>.

   What is the OPPOSITE of "turned Mary down?"

   A) made Mary stand up
   B) refused to help Mary
   C) agreed to help Mary
   D) said no to Mary

FACT/OPINION

3. Which statement contains an <u>opinion</u>?

   A) Mary made her own medicines.
   B) Mary was the best nurse of her time.
   C) Mary was born in Jamaica.
   D) Mary kept her hospital open until the end of the war.

IRRELEVANT DETAILS

4. Which statement is <u>least</u> important to the story of Mary Seacole?

   A) Although the army turned her down, Mary traveled to the war zone anyway.
   B) Mary spent all her own money on medicine and bandages.
   C) Mary kept her hospital open until the end of the war.
   D) Mary helped her mother with the cooking for the hotel.

WRITE ABOUT—

5. Was Mary Seacole's work more like that of a doctor or a nurse today? Give reasons for your answer.

3
THE AMERICANS WHO MET COLUMBUS

Christopher Columbus came to America 500 years ago. Most Europeans and Americans think of him as a great sailor and a great hero. But there was a dark side to what Columbus did. He and his men destroyed the very first people who welcomed him to America.

Columbus stopped first in the Caribbean islands. The first people he met were the Taino Indians. More than a million of these people lived on the large islands of Cuba, Hispaniola, and Puerto Rico. They were skilled farmers. They grew corn, cotton, and yams. They wove their cotton into cloth and made pottery. They were also skilled sailors. Their huge canoes could hold as many as 500 people.

The name *Taino* means "men of the good." To judge from what Columbus said about them, the name fit them. Columbus had run out of food on his trip from Spain. The friendly Tainos gave him all the food his men needed. Columbus was amazed. "Anything they have, they invite you to share, and they show much love," he wrote. The Tainos were peaceful, too. At first, Columbus believed they didn't have any weapons at all.

But Columbus and his men were greedy. Above all else, they wanted gold. And they wanted the Tainos to do all their work for them. "They will make excellent slaves," Columbus wrote. "They are very well fitted to do whatever is necessary." In 1494, he sent back a shipload of 500 Tainos to Spain. Two hundred died on the voyage. The rest were sold as slaves in Spain. One chief tried to make friends with Columbus by sending him gold masks. It didn't work. Columbus captured him anyway and sold him into slavery.

Columbus thought that the job of making slaves of all the Taino would be easy. He boasted that he could do the job with only fifty men. But the Tainos resisted. It was no use. The Spanish had horses and guns. One battle was fought between 200 Spaniards and 20,000 Tainos. The Tainos were badly beaten. Spanish guns were more deadly than Taino bows and arrows. The Spanish also had savage dogs, trained to tear their enemies to pieces.

After the battle, the Tainos tried to make peace. Columbus and his men demanded gold and cotton and more food. The Tainos gave him what they had. But they could not give Columbus everything that he and his men wanted.

One of the most important of the Taino chiefs was a man named Guarionex. He knew his people could not supply all the gold that the Spanish demanded. He went to Columbus with an offer. He said his people would plant all the food that the Spanish would ever eat. The Spanish refused. Only gold and Taino slaves would satisfy them.

Guarionex didn't want to fight, but other Taino chiefs called him a coward. They said he should fight back. Guarionex had a hard choice. If he attacked the Spaniards, he would probably lose. If he did nothing, his brothers would say he was no good as chief. Finally, he agreed to lead his Tainos into battle.

The Spaniards were led by Columbus's brother, Bartholomew. Bartholomew did not want to risk a battle. He knew that he would lose many men even if he won. Instead, he rode into Guarionex's village at night. He seized Guarionex and the other chiefs and took them away. Without their leaders, the Tainos were lost. Guarionex and other chiefs were sent as captives to Spain, but their ship sank. The Taino chiefs drowned along with the ship's crew.

Now the Tainos had no leaders. Their families had no food. They had to give their crops to the Spaniards. Some were worked to death. Others starved. Huge numbers died from the diseases that the Spanish brought from Europe. Today there are only about 2,000 descendants of the Tainos who welcomed Columbus.

Some of the Native Americans were more successful in fighting against the Spanish than Guarionex was. And some of the Spaniards were horrified at the Spanish treatment of the Tainos. Selection 17 in this book will tell you something about two of these people.

GLOSSARY

Hispaniola   The large island between Cuba and Puerto Rico. The countries of Haiti and the Dominican Republic are on the island.

savage   Wild and fierce.

yams   Sweet potatoes.

EXERCISES

MAIN IDEA

1. This selection tells why—

    A) the Taino people were defeated.
    B) Columbus did not like Guarionex.
    C) Christopher Columbus came to America.
    D) Taino chiefs killed each other.

COMPARE/CONTRAST

2. Which statement is true?

    A) The Spanish grew their own food, but the Taino didn't.
    B) The Tainos had no guns, but the Spanish did.
    C) The Spanish had always lived in America, but the Taino were newcomers.
    D) The Tainos were a lucky people, but the Spanish were unlucky.

FACT/OPINION

3. Which of the following statements is NOT an opinion?

    A) The name "people of the good" fit the Tainos.
    B) Guarionex was a coward.
    C) Columbus was a hero.
    D) The Tainos lived on Cuba, Hispaniola, and Puerto Rico.

DRAWING CONCLUSIONS

4. Guarionex led thousands of men. Bartholemew Columbus led only a few hundred men.

    These TWO statements explain why—

    A) Bartholemew sent Guarionex to Spain.
    B) Guarionex didn't want to fight the Spanish at first.
    C) Guarionex drowned.
    D) Bartholomew decided to capture Guarionex in a surprise night raid.

WRITE ABOUT—

5. Suppose you were advising Guarionex. What advice would you give him about how to deal with Columbus and the Spanish?

4
SINGING THE BLUES

Everybody knows a blues when they hear one. The blues is one of the great African-American gifts to the world's music. But what exactly is the blues? Listen to what the blues singers themselves say.

"Blues ain't nothing but a good man feelin' bad."

"Blues is poor man's heart disease."

"Blues is a cryin' woman whose man's gone off an' left her."

"Blues is all the things I wanted to do but never got around to doin'."

The blues is a feeling. It's the words that express that feeling. And it's the music that goes with those words.

Singers say different things about the blues. But one thing stays the same— the blues are personal. They describe how the singer feels. They may be sad. The singer feels like crying. But the blues can also be about feeling good. It depends on the singer. One of the great singers said about himself:

"My name is T-Bone Walker. That means I sing nothing but the blues. Give you that *good* feeling."

No one knows just how the blues began. There was plenty of African-American music before the blues. There were religious songs called spirituals that people sang together in church. There were work songs that workers sang together on the job to help a hard task go faster. There were dance songs, and story songs called ballads that told of the adventures of some hero or bad man. But none of these was the blues.

Then, about a hundred years ago, African-American singers started creating a new kind of music. The new songs were personal. They told of the singer's own feelings and troubles:

"I got the blues so bad I can feel them in the dark."

" Lord, I stand here wondering, will a match box hold my clothes?"

"I've got to keep moving—blues falling down like hail."

A new kind of music was being born. Soon the blues spread from singer to singer across the South. By the 1920's, jazz bands were playing blues tunes. Powerful-voiced black women were singing blues in clubs and theaters. Records brought blues songs and blues musical styles to African-American homes across the nation.

In the South, the home of the blues, country blues singers created new ways of playing the guitar while they sang. They slipped the broken-off neck of a bottle onto the third or fourth finger of their left hand. When they moved this bottleneck lightly across the guitar string, it gave out a singing, moaning sound that was perfect for blues. The guitar became as important as the singer.

In the 1930's and 1940's, many African-Americans moved north. Chicago became a new center of blues music. City life was faster than life in the South. Many urban blues musicians like T-Bone Walker, Muddy Waters, and the great B.B. King started playing their blues on electric guitars. An electric guitar gave the same kind of sound that the old bottleneck style did. In addition, it was louder. it could cut through the noise and excitement of a night club.

By the late 1940's, city blues musicians were performing in blues bands that might contain electric guitars, piano, harmonica, drums, and sometimes saxophones. Their music often had a strong, pounding beat that was good for dancing. People began to call it "rhythm and blues."

Even young white kids began listening to the new music and playing something like it themselves. Both white and black musicians began shaping the music to appeal to a teenage audience. The most successful was a young white truck driver named Elvis Presley. But many black musicians worked in the new style, too: Fats Domino, Little Richard, Chuck Berry. Rock 'n' roll had arrived. And the blues was at its heart.

Then, in the 1960's, tastes changed. High-energy soul singers became popular. The 1980's saw the rise of hip-hop and rap. The newest styles were angry and aggressive, built around flashy dance routines. The blues seemed to be dying.

But there are still lots of blues singers around. Some are young. Others have been around since the 1950's and before. And even old-style blues recordings have made a comeback. The recordings of a 1930's country blues singer, Robert Johnson, were reissued on CDs in the 1990's. They amazed the record industry by becoming national best sellers, more than 50 years after Johnson died.

The blues singers say it all: "The blues will never die."

GLOSSARY

aggressive   Tough and showing willingness to fight.

reissued   Put out again.

routines   Fancy dance steps.

JOHN LEE HOOKER

PHOTOFEST

John Lee Hooker, one of the greatest blues singers and guitarists. Born in Mississippi, Hooker moved north as a young man. In the 1950's he became the biggest name in Detroit blues. By the 1960's his powerful guitar style and dark, rich voice had made him an international blues star.

EXERCISES

SEQUENCE

1. Put the following in the correct order of time, from earliest to latest.

   A) earliest rap
   B) earliest rhythm and blues
   C) earliest rock and roll
   D) earliest country blues

WORD MEANING

2. The selection talks about <u>urban</u> blues musicians like T-Bone Walker, Muddy Waters, and B.B. King. What does "urban" mean?

   A) city
   B) country
   C) old-fashioned
   D) modern

CAUSE/EFFECT

3. How did early country blues guitarists get a moaning sound from their guitar?

   A) They moaned into the sound hole.
   B) They shook the guitar hard as they played it.
   C) They used special "moaner" guitar strings.
   D) They slid a bottleneck up and down the strings.

PREDICTING OUTCOMES

4. When both black and white musicians began shaping rhythm and blues to teenage tastes, the result was—

   A) country blues
   B) soul
   C) rock and roll
   D) urban blues

COMPARE/CONTRAST

5. What is the main difference between the blues and earlier African-American song styles?

    A) The blues is personal.
    B) The blues is faster.
    C) The blues is sung.
    D) The blues is older.

REFERENCE

6. Suppose you wanted to learn more about the blues. You would like to know how they started. You want to know more about blues singers. Which book would tell you most?

    A) an atlas
    B) an encyclopedia
    C) a dictionary
    D) an almanac

WRITE ABOUT—

7. Take any of the lines from a blues in the story, and write a second line to go with it. (The second line should rhyme with the first.)

5
THE CHINESE WHO BUILT A RAILROAD

Suppose you are in New York. You want to go to California. How do you get there? Today, there are many ways to go from New York to California. You can drive. You can take a bus, or a plane, or a train. But in 1863, you couldn't do any of these. There were no cars. There were no buses or planes. As for the railroads, they ended less than halfway across America. American trains started in the East. They carried people about a thousand miles. Then they stopped. No trains went as far as California.

America needed a railroad that went all the way from the East to the Pacific Ocean. In 1863, railroad companies began to build one. Men were hired and the work got started. One work crew began in Nebraska. They started to build a railroad going west. Another crew started in California and began a railroad heading east.

Work started first on the California railroad. But the owners had trouble getting workers. Only about 800 men signed on, and the owners needed 5,000. Workers disappeared. Many went to hunt for gold and silver in the mines of Nevada. The railroad owners didn't have enough workers to build the railroad. So they told their work boss to hire fifty Chinese laborers.

The boss didn't like this. Neither did the other workers. They said that the Chinese were too small and weak for the work. Their religion, their language, and their habits were strange. And in addition, they ate strange food—food that could never feed a real railroad worker.

The new Chinese workers came to the camp. Calmly, they set up their tents. They ate their supper and went to sleep. At dawn they got up and began to work. For twelve hours, they worked without a break.

It was soon clear that they worked faster than the white workers. They were amazingly strong. They didn't go on strike. They didn't get drunk on payday or stop working when the boss wasn't looking. They even set a new record for laying track. They laid ten miles of track on a single day.

The railroad boss liked what he saw. The Chinese crews got a lot of work done. He hired more Chinese workers. Soon he had hired nearly every Chinese worker in California. He sent to China for more. Before long, he had more than 6,000 Chinese employees.

What does it take to build a railroad through high mountains like the ones in California? One thing you need is gunpowder. It breaks big rocks into small pieces. But gunpowder is hard to use. It's dangerous. The white workers wouldn't touch it. So the Chinese were given this job.

The Chinese knew about gunpowder. After all, their ancestors had invented the stuff. But blasting the side of a mountain took skill and courage. First, the Chinese climbed up the mountains. Then they went over the mountain edge on ropes. Next, they made holes in the mountain rock. They filled the holes with gunpowder and lit the fuses. Now they had to move fast. They jerked their ropes to be pulled back up. They had to be quick. If they weren't, they could be blown to pieces.

Trains can't go over the tops of mountains. If there is no easy mountain pass, the railroad has to go through the mountain itself. Tunnels had to be blasted through the Sierra Nevada mountains. Making a tunnel is dangerous work. The Chinese crews made six of them.

The Chinese were working on the highest tunnel when winter hit. Winter is fierce in the Sierras. There were 44 blizzards that winter. One dumped more than 10 feet of snow on the mountains. In places, the snow was more than 60 feet deep. The Chinese kept on working. They had to dig roads under the snow to get to the mountain. There they blasted more than 1,600 feet through the solid rock to finish the tunnel.

One reason the Chinese could work so hard was because they were healthy. They had great stamina. Their way of living was much healthier than that of the white workers. Most white workers ate stale meat. They drank rough whisky that burned their stomachs. The Chinese treated their bodies with more respect. They ate fresh fish every day. The fish was brought in on the newly-built railroad from San Francisco. They ate the fish along with rice and vegetables. They drank tea, not whisky. All this helped the Chinese work longer and harder.

The railroad from California met up with the one from Nebraska in 1869. At last it was finished. Years later, one of its owners rode from coast to coast. He saw Chinese workers repairing the track. He said they were smaller than the other workers. But they worked like giants!

GLOSSARY

fuse   A slow-burning cord that is used to set off explosives.

Nebraska   A state in the middle of the United States.

Nevada   The state east of California.

stamina   The ability to do hard work for a long time without getting tired.

EXERCISES

WORD MEANINGS

1. The author says the Chinese had great <u>stamina</u>. People with great "stamina" —

   A) are unhealthy.
   B) sleep a lot and eat little.
   C) work for a long time.
   D) are often afraid.

MAKING JUDGMENTS

2. Why did the railroad bosses hire the first 50 Chinese workers?

   A) White workers cost too much.
   B) The white workers got into fights.
   C) There were too many white workers.
   D) White workers quit to look for gold.

SEQUENCE

3. Which came first?

   A) Fifty Chinese laborers were hired.
   B) Thousands of Chinese laborers were hired.
   C) Tunnels were blasted in the mountains.
   D) The new railroad was finished.

COMPARE/CONTRAST

4. The Chinese workers ate fresh fish and vegetables, and the white workers preferred stale meat.

   The Chinese workers drank tea and the white workers drank whiskey.

   These facts help explain why—

   A) The white workers were bigger than the Chinese workers.
   B) The Chinese workers had more stamina than the white workers.
   C) The Chinese workers were better with explosives than the white workers.
   D) The Chinese didn't quit to go mining, and the white workers did.

CAUSE/ EFFECT

5. What did the Chinese workers use gunpowder for?

   A) To kill people.
   B) To cook their food.
   C) To blast rocks away.
   D) To show they were brave.

WORD MEANINGS

6. The author says the white workers drank <u>rough</u> whisky. What is the meaning of "rough" in this sentence?

   A) Looking for a fight
   B) Cheap and bad
   C) Soft and calm
   D) Not level

WRITE ABOUT—

7. You have been hired to make a movie about the Chinese railroad workers. What event or incident would you most like to film? Why?

6
REVIEW QUESTIONS

I. WHAT'S IN THE PICTURE?

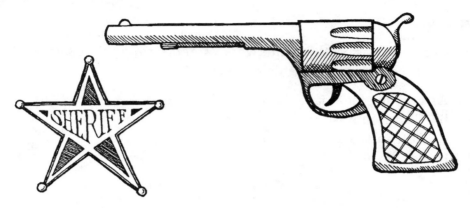

1. Who wore the two things in this picture?

   A) Guarionex
   B) Elfego Baca
   C) Christopher Columbus
   D) T-Bone Walker

II. WHO IS SPEAKING?

2. "Give me a wounded soldier, and I will help him."

   "A spoonful of this, two drops of that. Mix. Now drink it up. It will help your fever.

   "The army hospitals are terrible!"

   A) Elfego Baca
   B) Guarionex
   C) A blues singer
   D) Mary Seacole

3. "Give you that GOOD feeling."

"Ain't nothing but a good man feelin' bad."

"Lord, I stand here wondering, will a match box hold my clothes?"

A) Mary Seacole
B) A blues singer
C) Guarionex
D) A Chinese railroad builder

4. "We don't <u>have</u> any more gold."

"But if we attack, their guns will kill us."

"Come, be our guests, share this meal with us."

A) A Taino chief
B) Mary Seacole
C) A Chinese railroad builder
D) Elfego Baca

5. "I want outlaws to hear my steps a block away"

"My cousin Pedro worked here before me."

"I like to cook my own breakfast. Especially when there's 80 men shooting at me!"

A) Guarionex
B) Elfego Baca
C) Christopher Columbus
D) A Chinese railroad builder

III. WRITE ABOUT—

6. You have read three stories about people who took huge risks.

Pick one of them. Tell what you think was the most dangerous thing they did. Why do you feel this way?

Mary Seacole
Elfego Baca
Chinese railroad workers

Phillis Wheatley, the Boston poet who was born in Africa. She was seized by slave traders when she was only about seven years old and taken to America. Here her amazing talent for poetry made her famous. Even George Washington wanted to meet her.

7
THE AMERICAN POET FROM AFRICA

One of America's first poets was born in West Africa! Her name was Phillis Wheatley. She was taken from her home by slave traders when she was a little girl. She was only 7 or 8 years old. When she came to America she could not speak, read, or write English. But by the time she died, she was a famous poet.

We don't know how Phillis was captured in Africa. She didn't talk about it. But in 1761 she was kidnapped and put on a crowded slave ship. Many people on the ship died from hunger and disease. Somehow, Phillis survived. After six horrible weeks at sea, she arrived in the town of Boston.

In Boston, a middle-aged woman named Susannah Wheatley was looking for a personal maid. On the dock she saw a thin, frightened little girl wrapped in a dirty blanket. It was Phillis. Susannah bought the child as a slave and took her home.

Phillis learned English fast—very fast. Susannah realized Phillis was very smart. Usually, enslaved people were not taught to read. But Susannah taught Phillis. Then Phillis learned to write. The Wheatleys' daughter taught her.

Phillis worked hard for the Wheatley family. She spent her spare time reading. Two years after she came to America, she was reading the Bible. She was especially fond of poetry. She read the poems of many great English poets. She even learned Latin and read the works of the great poets who wrote in that language.

Phillis loved to write. When she was about seventeen, her first poem was published. People in Boston began to talk about her. Rich Boston families asked her to visit them. She read them her poems. The Wheatley family felt that they could no longer keep Phillis as a slave. They set her free.

At that time, America was still an English colony. Phillis traveled across the Atlantic to England. She was a big hit. Everyone wanted to meet her. She read her poems to large audiences. A book of her poems was published there.

Shortly after Phillis returned to America, the American Revolution began. General George Washington came to Boston to command the army there. Phyllis sent a poem to Washington. He was very impressed, and invited Phillis to visit him.

But after that, things did not go well for Phillis. She had no money. She was no longer a slave, but the Wheatleys had died, and she could no longer live in their house. She married and had three little children. The family was dirt poor. Phillis couldn't find work. They could not heat their small rooms. All three children died. Then Phillis died, too. She was only thirty.

By the time she died, Phillis had published over seventy poems. They are very different from the poems of today. In Phillis's time, poetry was very stiff and formal. It was filled with special "poetic" words that were never used outside of poetry. Poets used fancy language to say very simple things. Phillis wrote this kind of poetry very skillfully, but it is hard for us to read today.

Many of Phillis' poems are religious. She did not write about the problems of black people or about the country. But in one poem she gives a hint about what she must have felt when she was a slave:

> Should you, my lord, while you **peruse** (*read*) my song
> Wonder from whence my love of freedom sprung,
> I, young in life, by seeming cruel fate
> Was snatch'd from Afric's fancy'd happy seat...
> Such, such my case. And can I then but pray
> Others my never feel tyrannic sway?

In this poem, Phillis was writing to an English lord, the Earl of Dartmouth. He reads her poem and has a question. Why is freedom so important to Phillis? She answers him. She was free and happy when she was a child in Africa. Then one day, she was snatched from her home and sold into slavery. She loves freedom because she has known slavery, and she can only pray that it will not happen to others.

GLOSSARY

Afric's   A poetic way of writing "Africa's."

enslaved   Seized and made a slave.

Fancy'd   A poetic, old-fashioned way of saying "believed to be." Phillis is saying that she believes Africa to be a happy place, but she doesn't fully remember, since she was kidnapped as a child.

Latin   The language of the ancient Romans in Italy, about 2000 years ago.

seat   A poetic way of saying "place" or "location."

seeming   Apparently.

tyrannic sway   Rule by brutal rulers . (*Sway* means "rule," and *tyrannic* refers to a *tyrant*, or a cruel and brutal ruler.)

whence   From where.

EXERCISES

DRAWING CONCLUSIONS

1. What did the English think of Phillis Wheatley?

   A) They didn't like her.
   B) They never heard of her.
   C) They admired her.
   D) They had no opinion.

CAUSE/EFFECT

2. Why did George Washington ask Phillis to visit him?

   A) She had sent him a poem.
   B) He wanted information from her that would help him win the war.
   C) He had met her earlier and wanted to see her again.
   D) A friend had told him about her.

FACT/OPINION

3. Which statement is an <u>opinion</u>, not a fact?

   A) We don't know how Phillis was captured.
   B) Phillis' poem on her slavery is very moving.
   C) By the time she died, Phillis had published over 70 poems.
   D) Phyllis sent a poem to George Washington.

IRRELEVANT DETAILS

4. Which statement is <u>least</u> important to the story of Phillis Wheatley?

   A) She wrote many poems.
   B) She was on a dock when Mrs. Wheatley saw her.
   C) She wanted to read and write.
   D) She was enslaved for much of her life.

WRITE ABOUT—

5. Phillis' poem was about leaving home. Was there a time when you had to leave home for a while? Write a few sentences about how you felt.

8
THE NEW ORANGE OF LUE GIM GONG

Did you eat an orange today? Did you drink a glass of orange juice? Where did your orange come from? Many oranges come from Florida. Florida is famous for its oranges.

A hundred years ago, Florida didn't grow many oranges. The problem was the weather. Most of the time, even in winter, Florida has warm weather that is fine for oranges. But sometimes freezing weather comes down from the north. When these cold snaps came, the oranges died.

Today, Florida has a different kind of orange. It can live through the cold weather. This is the story of how Florida got this new orange. It is the story of a Chinese-American called Lue Gim Gong. With Lue's help, Florida became a land of oranges.

Lue was born in China. He was only 12 years old when he sailed to America. He went to live in Massachusetts. There, a Sunday-school teacher named Fanny Burlingame taught him to speak English.

Fanny loved plants. She had a large garden, and Lue helped in her greenhouses. He was only a teenager, but he knew a lot about working with plants. Back home in China, his mother had taught him many tricks. He knew how to graft plants. This meant he could take one type of plant and join it onto another. The new plant was like one parent in some ways and like the other parent in other ways.

Lue liked working for Fanny. But he had to stop. He became ill with a lung disease called tuberculosis. Doctors told him he had only a short time left to live. He went back home to China to die. But to everyone's surprise, he got better.

One day he had a letter from Fanny's family. They needed his help. The family now owned land in Florida. They were trying to grow oranges. However, the oranges weren't doing well. They were ruined by heavy rain or cold weather. The family wanted Lue to take care of their oranges. So Lue returned to America.

Lue decided to create a stronger orange. He used his skill at grafting. He grafted a Florida orange onto an orange from southern Europe. The new orange was a sweet, juicy fruit. Most important, it could stand the cold. It was named the Lue Gim Gong orange. In 1911, Lue's orange was awarded a medal.

Soon after this, Fanny Burlingame died. In her will, she left all her Florida land to Lue. Lue continued to grow his new oranges. He also created a new kind of grapefruit. He created new kinds of currants and peaches, too. He was a genius with plants.

Lue became famous. Thousands of people visited him. They came to see his gardens. Everyone wanted his new fruit.

Lue was a generous man, but he wasn't good at business. He gave his fruit away. He didn't take any money. Before long, other growers were rich, but Lue had no money left.

Lue was desperate. He wrote to a magazine read by all the fruit growers in Florida. He described what had happened to him. The magazine's readers felt sorry for him. They sent him money to help him solve his problems. Lue's home and garden were saved.

GLOSSARY

cold snaps Sudden, short periods of cold weather.

greenhouses Special "houses" made of glass, used for growing plants in places where the weather gets cold.

will A written statement that gives away a person's property after she or he is dead.

EXERCISES

SEQUENCE

1. Which came first?

    A) Lue made a new kind of Florida orange.
    B) Lue worked in Fanny's gardens in Massachusetts.
    C) Lue became ill with tuberculosis.
    D) Lue lost all his money.

MAKING JUDGMENTS

2. Lue won a medal because

    A) He cured tuberculosis.
    B) He was kind to people.
    C) He spoke English well.
    D) He made a new orange.

CAUSE/ EFFECT

3. Lue worked in Fanny's gardens. Why was he skilled at this work?

    A) He did not speak English.
    B) He read a lot of books..
    C) He had learned about plants from his mother.
    D) He was very generous to visitors.

WRITE ABOUT—

4. Think about some of the different things you eat. Pick one of them. How would you improve it, if you could?

9
EDDIE MIRANDA LOOKS AT NEW YORK

This a true story. It was written by Eddie Miranda, a young woman who came to New York City from the island of Puerto Rico. In this selection, she tells what it is like to live in in the largest city in the United States.

My family and I came to New York City from Puerto Rico. Here it is more exciting. You can have a better life here. But I don't know if we'll stay.

Life here is different. The climate of Puerto Rico is better. It is much warmer there. We can do a lot outdoors. The weather here is hard. Some of my friends went back because of the New York weather. It is too cold.

The culture of New York City is totally different. We live in a big building. We are always with people from different nationalities. We share our life with different people. We pick up customs from other countries. After a while, we are totally different people. I do not like this.

Language is one of the biggest problems. Because of language, it is hard to get a job. In order to survive, we must work. So we have to take any kind of job. This hurts our status.

Also, many people treat us like foreigners. We have a right to live here and work here. People do not know this. They ask to see our green cards. They ask for work permits. We often get mad at how we are treated.

We lived in a small place in Puerto Rico. Everyone knew my parents. So we had to be quiet. We had to do things right. Here it is different. Nobody knows who you are. People say, "Do what you want. Who cares?" So people sometimes act crazy here. In Puerto Rico, we act better and I prefer this.

In spite of everything, many of us like it here. Most of us are happy to be in New York.

GLOSSARY

green card   A card that permits a person from another country to live and work in the United States

---

EXERCISES

COMPARE/CONTRAST

1. What does Eddie prefer about Puerto Rico?

   A) It is warmer.
   B) It is quieter.
   C) It is more exciting.
   D) It is more beautiful.

COMPARE/ CONTRAST

2. What does Eddie prefer about New York?

   A) It is cooler.
   B) You can speak English.
   C) You meet more people.
   D) It is more exciting.

MAKING JUDGMENTS

3. How does Eddie feel when someone asks for her work permit?

   A) pleased
   B) angry
   C) worried
   D) afraid

VOCABULARY DEVELOPMENT

4. In New York, Eddie meets people from many countries. Which words in the selection have the same meaning as <u>people from many countries</u>.

   A) different nationalities
   B) Puerto Ricans
   C) Spanish speakers
   D) strangers

WRITE ABOUT—

5. Think about the town or place where you live. What would you miss most about it if you went to live in another place?

36

10
ELIZABETH ECKFORD
GOES TO SCHOOL

In the 1950's, it was dangerous for African-Americans to stand up for their rights. It was just as dangerous for children as it was for grown-ups. On September 4, 1957, Elizabeth Eckford found this out the hard way.

The Supreme Court said in 1954 that it was against the law to make black and white students go to separate schools. But in the Deep South, nothing changed. Finally, in 1957, a U.S. court ordered Central High School in Little Rock, Arkansas, to open its doors to nine black students. Elizabeth Eckford was going to be one of them.

Governor Faubus of Arkansas didn't want black children in white schools. He claimed that blood would be shed if the nine children entered Central High. He ordered out the Arkansas National Guard. The National Guard is a kind of state army controlled by the governor, and Governor Faubus was really using it to defy the U.S. court order.

But Elizabeth thought the Guardsmen would protect her when she went to school. She was dead wrong. Here is how she described what happened that frightening first day.

When I got right in front of the school, I went up to a guard again. But this time he just looked straight ahead and didn't move to let me pass him. I didn't know what to do. Then I looked and saw that the path leading to the front entrance was a little further ahead. So I walked until I was right in front of the path to the front door.

I stood looking at the school—it looked so big! Just then the guards let some white students go through.

The crowd was quiet. I guess they were waiting to see what was going to happen. When I was able to steady my knees, I walked up to the guard who had let the white students in. He too didn't move. When I tried to squeeze past him, he raised his bayonet and then the other guards closed in and they raised their bayonets.

They glared at me with a mean look and I was very frightened and didn't know what to do. I turned around and the crowd came toward me.

They moved closer and closer. Somebody started yelling, "Lynch her! Lynch her!"

I tried to see a friendly face somewhere in the mob—someone who maybe would help. I looked into the face of an old woman and it seemed a kind face, but when I looked at her again, she spat on me.

They came closer, shouting, "No nigger bitch is going to get in our school. Get out of here!"

I turned back to the guards but their faces told me I wouldn't get help from them. Then I looked down the block and saw a bench at the bus stop. I thought, "If I can only get there I will be safe." I don't know why the bench seemed such a safe place to me, but I started walking toward it. I tried to close my mind to what they were shouting, and kept saying to myself, "If I can only make it to the bench I will be safe."

When I finaly got there, I don't think I could have gone another step. I sat down and the mob crowded up and began shouting all over again. Someone hollered, "Drag her over to this tree! Let's take care of the nigger." Just then a white man sat down beside me, put his arm around me and patted my shoulder, He raised my chin and said, "Don't let them see you cry."

Then, a white lady—she was very nice—she came over to me on the bench. She spoke to me but I don't remember now what she said. She put me on the bus and sat next to me. She asked me my name and tried to talk to me but I don't think I answered. I can't remember much about the bus ride, but the next thing I remember I was standing in front of the School for the Blind where Mother works.

I thought, "Maybe she isn't here. But she has to be here!" So I ran upstairs, and I think some teachers tried to talk to me, but I kept running until I reached Mother's classroom.

Mother was standing at the window with her head bowed, but she must have sensed I was there because she turned around. She looked as if she had been crying, and I wanted to tell her I was all right. But I couldn't speak. She put her arms around me and I cried.

Three weeks after school opened, President Eisenhower ordered units of the U.S. Army to enforce the U.S. court order. Protected by the Army, Elizabeth Eckford and eight other black students entered Central High.

GLOSSARY

bayonet   A long knife attached to the end of a gun barrel.

lynch   Kill, usually because of race hatred.

ELIZABETH ECKFORD

On her first day at high school, 15-year-old Elizabeth Eckford walks through a mob of whites screaming "Lynch her! Lynch her!" The year was 1957, and Elizabeth was one of the first nine black students to go to all-white Central High School in Little Rock, Arkansas.

EXERCISES

MAIN IDEA

1. The main idea of this selection is that—

   A) Elizabeth was comforted by her mother.
   B) Elizabeth felt safer when she sat on the bench.
   C) Elizabeth had a terrifying experience on her first day at high school.
   D) Elizabeth got no help from the Guards.

SEQUENCE

2. Put these events in order:

   A) A woman sat down next to Elizabeth in the bus.
   B) Elizabeth walked upstairs at the School for the Blind.
   C) The Guardsmen raised their bayonets.
   D) The crowd shouted threats.

COMPARE/CONTRAST

3. Elizabeth met two women. They both seemed kind at first. How did she learn that one of these women wasn't kind at all?

   A) The woman said mean things.
   B) The woman took Elizabeth's seat on the bus.
   C) The woman spat at her.
   D) The woman threw a stone at her.

CAUSE/EFFECT

4. Why had Guardsmen been placed in front of Central High?

   A) to prevent black students from entering
   B) to keep the crowd in order
   C) to protect black students
   D) to prevent white students from entering

FACT/OPINION

5. Which of the following statements is NOT an opinion?

   A) The crowd was vicious and evil.
   B) The Guardsmen didn't do their job right.
   C) Two white people talked to Elizabeth.
   D) Elizabeth was lucky to survive that day.

WRITE ABOUT-

6. Were you ever faced with something unfair that you couldn't do anything about? Tell about it.

11
THE ZOOT SUIT RIOTS OF LOS ANGELES

In 1943, America was at war. Los Angeles was full of sailors. Some were home on leave. Others were waiting to go overseas. On June 7, 1943, some of these sailors started fights. They looked for young men in zoot suits. As soon as they saw a zoot suit, they attacked.

What was going on? What were these fights about? What were zoot suits? Let's go back in time and find out.

Many Mexican-Americans live in California. A few families have lived there for hundreds of years. Most, however, came after 1900. Many white Americans looked down on the newcomers. They looked down on people who had a different ways of life. They made fun of Mexican-Americans who didn't understand English or who didn't speak it the way they did. When America entered the war, things got worse.

Mexican-American teenagers got angry. They were Americans, too! They had plenty to be proud of. They formed their own clubs. They called themselves Pachucos. The name came from the Mexican city of Pachuca, north of Mexico City. Pachuca is famous for its bright clothes. The Mexican-American teenagers had their own fashions. They wore special clothes called zoot suits.

Zoot suits looked like ordinary suits gone crazy. The pants were cut very full and loose, but tight at the ankle. The waist was high, starting just below the chest. Zoot suit jackets had very wide, padded shoulders and hung down below the knees. A flat hat with a very wide brim was often part of the outfit. So was a long, hanging gold watch chain. The Pachucos had their own hair style, too. They cut their hair in a duck-tail.

The zoot suit riots began the evening of June 3. No one knows how they started. The newspapers reported that some sailors tried to pick up some Mexican-American girls. Then a group of Pachucos attacked the sailors. Maybe it happened that way, and maybe it didn't. No one knows for sure how the fights started. But soon there were fights all over the city.

Sailors attacked anyone wearing a zoot suit. Mexican-Americans in zoot suits were attacked in bars and movie houses. Their suits were ripped off. Then they were beaten up. There were hundreds of fights between sailors and Pachucos.

The police didn't stop the fights. Newspapers printed untrue stories that put all the blame on the Mexican-American kids. One newspaper headline said, "Zooters Planning to Attack More Servicemen." By June 7, Los Angeles was in the middle of a full-scale race riot.

The Mexican government helped to stop the riots. Yes, the Mexican government! Mexico persuaded the United States to control the rioting sailors.

The governor of California wanted to understand what happened. He asked some important citizens to find out. Their report said that race hatred caused the riots.

It's an ugly story. It made the Anglo citizens of California feel ashamed. It made Mexican-Americans very angry. Many people still remember what happened. It took many years for the anger to fade.

GLOSSARY

brim The part of a hat that sticks out all around.

padded Stuffed with cloth to make it seem bigger.

riots Street fights between large groups of people, often people of different races or different backgrounds.

EXERCISES

CAUSE/ EFFECT

1. Why did young Mexican-Americans like to wear zoot suits?

   A) They were sharp-looking and colorful.
   B) They didn't cost much.
   C) They were easy to clean.
   D) They looked like sailors' uniforms.

MAIN IDEA

2. This selection is mainly about—

   A) what happens when you wear a zoot suit.
   B) World War II.
   C) Mexican-American pride.
   D) what happened because of prejudice against Mexican-Americans.

TRUE/FALSE

3. Which is true?

   A) The Pachucos were sailors.
   B) Most Anglos got in fights with Pachucos.
   C) Pachucos took their name from a Mexican city.
   D) The Governor wore a zoot suit.

SEQUENCE

4. Which came first?

   A) Sailors and Pachucos fought.
   B) Newspapers printed untrue stories about Pachucos.
   C) The Governor tried to learn about the riots.
   D) The U.S. went to war.

SETTING

5. Most of the action in this selection takes place in—

   A) wartime Los Angeles.
   B) Washington, D.C.
   C) Mexico City.
   D) the city of Pachuca in Mexico.

CAUSE/EFFECT

6. The report to the governor said that—

   A) the real cause of the riots was race prejudice.
   B) the riots were caused by the Mexican government.
   C) the riots were started by Pachucos who tried to pick up some girls.
   D) The riots started in the town of Pachuca.

WRITE ABOUT—

7. Is there anything you like to wear that someone else disapproves of? What is it, and how do you handle the situation?

12
REVIEW QUESTIONS

I. CROSSWORD

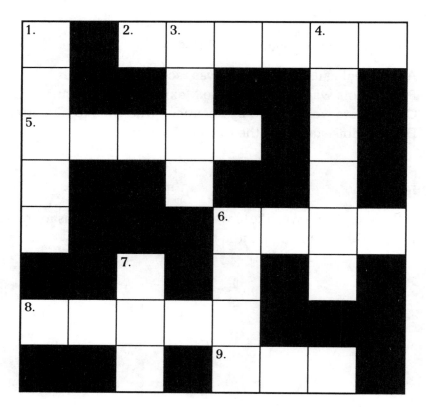

CLUES ACROSS

2. Lue Gim Gong created a new one.
5. Mary Seacole was one.
6. A ____ woman spat at Elizabeth Eckford.
8. First people Columbus met.
9. Elfego was a ___ gun.

CLUES DOWN

1. Blues are (usually) sad ____.
3. Danger (*e.g.*, from rail building)
4. They terrified Elizabeth.
6. Fighting between sailors and Zoot Suiters was called this.
7. Billy the ___ taught Elfego.

II. MAP

Here is a map of the United States. There are four places marked on the map. Each place is connected with someone in the selections you've just read. Match the person or people with the place.

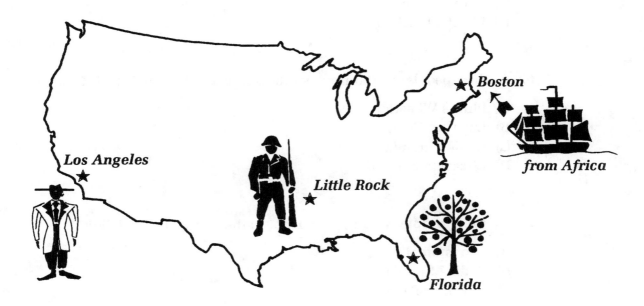

1. THE BOAT FROM AFRICA

   A) Lue Gim Gong
   B) Phillis Wheatley
   C) Elizabeth Eckford
   D) Eddie Miranda

2. LOS ANGELES

   A) Phillis Wheatley
   B) Elizabeth Eckford
   C) Zoot Suiters
   D) Fanny Burlingame

3. FLORIDA

   A) Lue Gim Gong
   B) Phillis Wheatley
   C) Elizabeth Eckford
   D) Eddie Miranda

4. LITTLE ROCK

   A) Zoot Suiters
   B) Susannah Wheatley
   C) Lue Gim Gong
   D) Elizabeth Eckford

III. ODD ONE OUT, or WHO DOESN'T BELONG?

5. All these people wrote about themselves EXCEPT—

   A) Phillis Wheatley
   B) Zoot Suiters
   C) Eddie Miranda
   D) Elizabeth Eckford

6. All these people were born outside the continental United States EXCEPT—

   A) Phillis Wheatley
   B) Lue Gim Gong
   C) Eddie Miranda
   D) Elizabeth Eckford

7. All these people were written about in the newspapers EXCEPT—

   A) Zoot suiters
   B) Eddie Miranda
   C) Governor Faubus
   D) Elizabeth Eckford

IV. MISSING PERSONS

In each of the passages below, a person's name is hidden. It may be either a first name or a last name. For example, in the passage:

*I must feed the soldiers. I'll u**se a cole**slaw salad, lots of potatoes, and some roasted meat.*

The underlined letters spell the name *Seacole*. The passage itself also gives you a clue. It talks about feeding soldiers, and Mary Seacole was an nurse who cured and fed wounded soldiers.

Now see if you can find the missing names in these passages. When you find them, underline them. And remember, there will also be a clue about the hidden person.

8. On the farm I ran daily. But when I came to New York, things changed.

9. At first, she was a wreck. For days, she shook with fear. Then slowly she forgot the horrible events at the school.

10. My troubles are over. I'm going on growing fruit.

48

13
THE PLAYER WHO BROKE BASEBALL'S COLOR BARRIER

April 9, 1947, is a special day for baseball. It was the first day that an African-American played baseball for a major league team. The team was the Brooklyn Dodgers. The man was Jackie Robinson.

Jackie was born in Georgia in 1919. He lived there for a few years. Then the family moved to California. Jackie was always good at games. He was the one the other boys always wanted to beat. His older brother Mack was also a fine athlete. When Jackie was 17, Mack ran in the Olympic Games. He finished second and won a silver medal.

Jackie decided he would be a star too. In college, he was both a star baseball player and a star football player. But in 1941 America entered World War II. Jackie joined the army. He became an officer, a good one. He knew how to lead his men. He took care of his soldiers. The army put him on its football team. But the other side wouldn't play against a black player. The army didn't stick up for Jackie. After that, he refused to play on the army team.

After the army, Jackie wanted to play baseball. He couldn't play in the major leagues. In those days, only white players played for the majors. So Jackie played baseball in the Negro leagues. It was a tough life. The men played all year round. Blacks were barred from many hotels. Restaurants served whites only. The black teams often had to eat and sleep on their buses. But they put up with it. They loved baseball.

Why didn't blacks play on white teams? It wasn't against the law. The white team owners gave a reason for the color barrier. They said black players weren't good enough. But this wasn't true. The real reason was racism. Most baseball fans were white. The team owners were afraid white fans would stay away if blacks played. They were also afraid that white players wouldn't accept a black man on their team.

The first man to realize this was not true was Branch Rickey. He was the owner of the Brooklyn Dodgers. Rickey knew black players were good. He knew Jackie Robinson was great. Jackie could help the Brooklyn Dodgers win the championship. Rickey wanted Robinson to be the first player to break the color barrier. There was one thing Rickey had to find out. He knew many white fans and players didn't like blacks. They would boo and shout dirty names. Could Robinson take it?

GLOSSARY

Brooklyn Dodgers   A National League baseball team, now the Los Angeles Dodgers.

color barrier   The customs or unwritten rules that barred African-Americans from major-league baseball and other sports.

major leagues   Two groups of baseball teams that play in the largest stadiums and that compete for the World Series championship each year.

rookie   A first-year player.

triumph   A great success.

Sometimes fans yell at ball players. The players must keep playing. They cannot hit the fans. They cannot get too angry to play well. Could Robinson do it? Did he have the guts to play ball when the fans cursed him? Rickey tested Jackie. He cursed him and called him "Nigger Boy." Robinson passed the test. He held himself back. He was hired.

Robinson started playing. It was tough. It was every bit as tough as Rickey expected. Many fans were mean and nasty. Some yelled, "Go back to the jungle." Many of Jackie's teammates were unfriendly. At first, he didn't play well.

Pee Wee Reese was a white player on the Dodgers' team. One day, when things were really bad, Reese stopped the game. He went over to his black teammate and put his arm round Jackie's shoulders. The two men talked for a while. The other players saw this. Most of them followed Pee Wee's lead. They became more friendly towards Jackie. The Dodger fans changed, too. Now they were pleased to have Jackie on their team.

Jackie's game improved. He began to hit like a champ. He ran like a star. He showed the fans what black baseball was like. The players in the Negro Leagues were great at fast base running. They played a tricky, fun game. It really turned the fans on. Jackie brought this style of playing to the Dodgers.

Sometimes, players on the other teams tried to get rough. This was a mistake. Jackie had been a football star, and he could play rough too. Other players learned the hard way not to mess with him. At the end of his first season, Jackie was named Rookie of the Year.

continued on p. 52

JACKIE ROBINSON

Jackie Robinson, the first African-American in major league baseball. This photo is taken from The Jackie Robinson Story, *a movie about Robinson's life in which he starred.*

For ten more years, Robinson played with the Dodgers. The team won the league championship six times. 1955 saw their greatest triumph. In that year the Brooklyn Dodgers won their first World Series. In that series, Jackie was a star. In one game, he even stole home!

Jackie proved black players were good. Very quickly, other baseball teams hired black players. By the time Robinson retired, most teams had black players.

In 1962, Robinson was picked for baseball's Hall of Fame. He died ten years later.

EXERCISES

MAIN IDEA

   1. This selection is mainly about—

      A) the rules of baseball.
      B) Army life.
      C) the first black major league player.
      D) the Brooklyn team.

SEQUENCE

   2. Put these events in order, from earliest to latest.

      A) The Dodgers won the World Series.
      B) Jackie played in the Negro Leagues.
      C) Branch Rickey called Jackie "nigger boy."
      D) Pee Wee Reese put his arm around Jackie's shoulder.

CHARACTER DESCRIPTION

   3. In Branch Rickey's opinion, Jackie Robinson was—

      A. tough
      B. stupid
      C. lazy
      D. young

CONTEXT CLUES

4. When the author says Jackie Robinson "held himself back," this means that he—

   A. turned around.
   B. had a painful injury.
   C. started a fight.
   D. controlled himself.

MULTIPLE MEANING

5. The army didn't <u>stick up for</u> Jackie. Which word means the same thing as "stick up for"?

   A. curse
   B. pay
   C. support
   D. like

WRITE ABOUT

6. Pretend you are Branch Rickey. You want to help prepare Jackie Robinson for his career in the major leagues Write a list of some of the things you want to warn him about.

14
THE MIGRANTS, PART 1

This is the first part of a short story about a Mexican family in California. It is taken from a short story called "The Circuit." The author is Dr. Francisco Jiménez, a writer and college professor in California.

The family in Dr. Jiménez' story are migrant farm workers. A MIGRANT is a person who moves from one place to another. A MIGRANT WORKER is a worker who moves from one farm to another, picking the crops as they become ready. Dr. Jiménez grew up in a family like this.

The story is told by Panchito, a young boy. Through his eyes, you see what life was like for his family. You also see what life was like for Dr. Jiménez when he was a boy.

As we drove home Papa did not say a word. With both hands on the wheel, he stared at the dirt road. My older brother, Roberto, was also silent. He leaned his head back and closed his eyes. Once in a while he cleared from his throat the dust that blew in from outside.

Yes, it was that time of year. When I opened the front door to the shack, I stopped. Everything we owned was neatly packed in carboard boxes. I sat down on a box. The thought of having to move to Fresno and knowing what was in store for me there brought tears to my eyes.

That night I could not sleep. I lay in bed thinking about how much I hated this move.

. . . Papá parked the car out in front and left the motor running. "Listo," he yelled. Without saying a word, Roberto and I began to carry the boxes out to the car. Roberto carried the two big boxes and I carried the two smaller ones. Papa then threw the mattress on top of the car roof and tied it with ropes to the front and rear bumpers.

Everything was packed except Mama's pot. It. had many dents and nicks, and the more dents and nicks it acquired the more Mama liked it. "Mi olla," she used to say proudly.

I held the front door open as Mama carefully carried out her pot by both handles, making sure not to spill the cooked beans. When she got to the car, Papa reached out to help her with it. Roberto opened the rear car door and Papa gently placed it on the floor behind the front seat. All of us then climbed in. Papa sighed, wiped the sweat off his forehead with his sleeve, and said wearily: "Es todo."

As we drove away, I felt a lump in my throat. I turned around and looked at our little shack for the last time.

At sunset we drove into a labor camp near Fresno. Since Papa did not speak English, Mama asked the camp foreman if he needed any more workers. "We don't need no more," said the foreman, scratching his head. "Check with Sullivan down the road. Can't miss him. He lives in a big house with a fence around it."

When we got there, Mama walked up to the house. "We have work! Mr. Sullivan said we can stay there the whole season," she said gasping and pointing to an old garage near the stables.

The garage was worn out by the years. It had no windows. That night, by the light of a kerosene lamp, we unpacked and cleaned our new home. Roberto swept away the loose dirt, leaving the hard ground. Papa plugged the holes in the walls with old newspapers and tin can tops. Mama fed my little brothers and sisters. Papa and Roberto then brought in the mattress and placed it on the far corner of the garage. "Mama, you and the little ones sleep on the mattress. Roberto, Panchito, and I will sleep outside under the trees," Papa said.

In the next selection, you will read the rest of Panchito's story.

GLOSSARY

Es todo   "That's all."

kerosene   a liquid , somewhat like gasoline, used as fuel in lamps and
    stoves.

Listo   "Ready."

Mi olla   "My jar."

EXERCISES

IDIOM

1. Panchito says he felt <u>a lump in his throat</u>. A person with a lump in his throat feels—
   A) sick
   B) sad
   C) tired
   D) angry

PREDICTING OUTCOMES

2. Panchito always knows that his family is about to move when—

   A) his father starts to talk in Spanish.
   B) his brother doesn't say anything.
   C) he sees everything they own packed in cardboard boxes.
   D) he and his father sleep under the trees

MAIN IDEA

3. This selection is about—

   A) a migrant family on the move.
   B) cleaning house.
   C) work and school.
   D) Mama's old cooking pot.

VOCABULARY DEVELOPMENT

4. Mama's cooking pot <u>acquired</u> lots of dents and nicks. Which word has the same meaning as "acquired"?

   A) cleaned
   B) got
   C) fixed
   D) hid

COMPARE/ CONTRAST

5. Mama spoke to the camp foreman at Fresno and to Mr. Sullivan. They had different answers for her. What was different?

   A) The camp foreman had work for them.
   B) Mr. Sullivan had work for them.
   C) There was nowhere for them to stay at the camp.
   D) Mr. Sullivan didn't need any help.

FACT/OPINION

6. Which statement is a <u>fact</u>?

   A) There's nothing worse than sleeping on the ground.
   B) The garage was a horrible place to live.
   C) The family cleaned the garage.
   D) The life of a migrant worker is miserable.

WRITE ABOUT

7. Suppose you had to move several times a year all the time, like the family in the story. List 5 personal possessions that you would always take with you.

15
THE MIGRANTS, PART 2

This is the second part of *"THE MIGRANTS,"* Dr. Francisco Jiménez' story about a family of Mexican farmworkers in California.

Early next morning Mr. Sullivan showed us where his crop was, and after breakfast, Papa, Roberto, and I headed for the vineyard . . . .

We took a break to eat lunch. It was past two o'clock and we sat underneath a large walnut tree that was on the side of the road . . . . Suddenly I noticed Papa's face turn pale as he looked down the road. "Here comes the school bus," he whispered loudly in alarm . . . . Roberto and I ran and hid in the vineyards. We did not want to get in trouble for not going to school. The neatly dressed boys about my age got off. They carried books under their arms . . . .

It was Monday, the first week of November. The grape season was over and I could now go to school. I woke up early that morning [happy at]...the thought of not going to work and of starting sixth grade for the first time that year. Since I could not sleep, I decided to get up and join Papa and Roberto at breakfast. I sat at the table across from Roberto, but I kept my head down. I did not want him to look up and face him. I knew he was sad. He was not going to school today. He was not going tomorrow, or next week, or next month. He would not go until the cotton season was over, and that was sometime in February . . . .

Two hours later, around eight o'clock, I stood by the side of the road waiting for school bus number twenty. When it arrived I climbed in. Everyone was busy either talking or yelling. I sat in an empty seat in the back.

When the bus stopped in front of the school, I felt very nervous. I . . . walked to the principal's office. When I entered I heard a woman's voice say: "May I help you?" I was startled. I had not heard English for months . . . . Finally, after struggling for English words, I managed to tell her that I wanted to enroll in the sixth grade. After answering many questions, I was led to the classroom.

Mr. Lema, the sixth grade teacher, greeted me and assigned me a desk. He then introduced me to the class. I was so nervous and scared at that moment when everyone's eyes were on me that I wished I were with Papa and Roberto picking cotton . . . .

During recess I went into the rest room and opened my English book to page 125. I began to read in a low voice, pretending I was in class. There were many words I did not know. I closed the book and headed back to the classroom.

Mr. Lema was sitting at his desk correcting papers. When I entered he looked up at me and smiled. I felt better. I walked up to him and asked if he could help me with the new words. "Gladly," he said . . . .

One Friday during lunch hour Mr. Lema asked me..."Do you like music?" . . . "Yes, I like corridos," I answered. He then picked up a trumpet, blew on it and handed it to me . . . . "How would you like to learn how to play it?" he asked.

That day I could hardly wait to get home to tell Papa and Mama the great news. As I got off the bus, my little brothers and sisters ran up to meet me. They were yelling and screaming. I thought they were happy to see me, but when I opened the door to our shack, I saw that everything we owned was neatly packed in cardboard boxes.

GLOSSARY

corridos   Old-style songs and ballads.

enroll in   Join by putting your name on a list.

EXERCISES

DRAWING CONCLUSIONS

1. Why didn't Roberto start school along with Panchito?

   A) He was a bad student.
   B) He had already finished school.
   C) He had to help his father pick cotton.
   D) He went to a different school.

VOCABULARY DEVELOPMENT

2. Panchito says, "Mr. Lema, the teacher, gave me a desk." Which word means the same as "gave"?
   A) built
   B) painted
   C) greeted
   D) assigned

OUTLINING

3. Look at this outline of events in the story:

   I) Panchito hid from the school bus.
   II) Panchito went to school.
   III) ....
   IV) Panchito's brothers and sisters were yelling.

   What belongs in the missing part?

   A) Mr. Sullivan showed where his crop was.
   B) Panchito ate lunch under a walnut tree.
   C) Panchito picked grapes.
   D) Panchito asked Mr. Lema to help him.

IDIOM

4. The selection says Panchito struggled for English words. Someone who <u>struggles for words</u>—

   A) fights his teacher.
   B) wins English prizes.
   C) finds it hard to speak.
   D) drops out of school.

MAKING JUDGMENTS

5. Why did Panchito read his English book during recess?

   A) He did not want to learn Spanish.
   B) He wanted to practice his English.
   C) He did not want to go home.
   D) Papa told him to reead the book.

PREDICTING OUTCOMES

6. What do you think will happen after the end of the story?

   A) The family is going to move again.
   B) Mr. Lema will teach Panchito how to play the trumpet.
   C) Roberto will go to school, too.
   D) Panchito's father will be offered a steady job.

WRITE ABOUT—

7. Was Panchito happy at the end of the story? Write a sentence to explain your answer.

Jack Johnson, the first black heavyweight boxing champ. He is still considered to be one of the greatest boxers of all time

16
THE GREATEST FIGHTER

The man that many people consider the greatest boxer of all time was born in 1878 in Galveston, Texas. His name was Jack Johnson, and he was the first African-American to win the heavyweight boxing championship of the world.

Johnson left school after fifth grade and did odd jobs. He also found time to beg, gamble, and fight. He was the best boxer in town when he was still a teenager.

One day, he heard there was going to be a big boxing tournament. It would be held in Springfield. Springfield was many miles away. Jack had no money. He couldn't buy a train ticket. So he traveled without one. He jumped on a freight train and hid behind some packages. There was nothing to eat, and he didn't get much sleep. He arrived just before fight time. He was tired and hungry, but that didn't stop him. He knocked out four fighters. His boxing career had begun.

Before long Johnson was a well-known fighter. People talked about him all the time. They came from all over to see him fight. Johnson fought every month. In five years, he only lost twice. Everyone knew he was great. But the best white boxers refused to fight him. They were afraid.

Finally, in 1908, the champion, Tommy Burns, agreed to box him. Johnson easily outpunched Burns. He teased him while he did so. "Look, Tommy," he said, "I'm going to hit you right in the belly." And he did just that. He knocked Burns out, and became the first black heavyweight world champion.

Having a black champion made many white Americans very unhappy. Johnson upset them in other ways, too. He drove fancy cars. He was always speeding. He had a lot of white girlfriends, and he later married one of them. Angry white Americans searched for a "Great White Hope" to win back the boxing crown. They finally persuaded Jim Jeffries, a former world champ, to come out of retirement.

Jeffries was a great fighter who had never lost a match. He had never even been knocked down. But he was out of shape, and no match for Johnson. Jeffries tried to hide from Jack's punches by clinging to him. Johnson just teased him: "Oh, Mr. Jeff, don't love me so." Then he knocked Jeffries out. Jeffries earned almost $200,000, but he later said that the beating he took wasn't worth it.

Beating Jeffries made Johnson more unpopular than ever. He was arrested. The arrest was not fair. Johnson fled to Europe. There he was treated like a king. He traveled to Spain and for a short time became a bullfighter. He killed three bulls in his first bullfight.

In the end, Johnson came home. But he had lost his edge as a fighter. He was knocked out by a clumsy giant named Jess Willard. He went to jail for nearly a year. He didn't waste time while he was there. Johnson was a smart man. He invented a new kind of monkey wrench. This wrench was easier to use. It was also easier to repair.

After he got out of jail, Johnson went back to fighting. He was a pro boxer for 12 more years, and he was still strong when he retired from the ring. Many boxers get broken noses. Their faces have scars from old cuts. Not Jack Johnson. You couldn't tell from his face that he'd ever been a boxer. It was smooth and unmarked. It wasn't broken up like other ex-fighters.

Jack didn't fight in the 1930's. But he was busy. He lectured. He taught boxing. He sold stock. In addition, he acted in movies and raced cars.

Johnson drove very fast. People were afraid to drive with him. They said it was safer to fight him than to drive in his car. He had a lot of auto accidents. He finally died in one in 1946.

Back in 1927, *Ring* Magazine, the magazine of boxing and wrestling, named Johnson "the greatest heavyweight boxer of all time." Many people think that this opinion is still true.

GLOSSARY

clinging   Holding very close.

monkey wrench   A tool for holding and twisting things that can be adjusted for different size objects.

odd jobs   Short jobs of different kinds.

stock   Shares in the ownership of a company.

EXERCISES

COMPARE/CONTRAST

1. What was the difference between Johnson's face and the faces of most ex-boxers?

   A) His face was very wrinkled.
   B) His face was smooth and unmarked.
   C) His face always looked tired.
   D) His face was badly bruised.

FIGURATIVE LANGUAGE

2. The author says that white Americans wanted to win back the boxing crown. This means they thought that—

   A) a white boxer should be champion.
   B) a white boxer should earn lots of money.
   C) a white boxer should not fight a black boxer.
   D) a white boxer should teach young boxers.

MAIN IDEA

3. This selection is mainly about—

   A) Jack Johnson's trip in a freight car
   B) an African-American world boxing champion
   C) a famous boxer's year in jail
   D) fighting bulls

OUTLINING

4. Complete the outline.

   I. Johnson became world champion.

   II. ....

   III. Johnson fled to Europe.

   IV. Johnson retired from boxing.

   A) Johnson killed three bulls.
   B) Johnson knocked out four boxers in one tournament.
   C) Johnson defeated Jim Jeffries.
   D) Johnson acted in movies.

FACT/ FICTION

5. Which statement contains an <u>opinion</u>?

   A) Johnson had car accidents.
   B) Johnson invented a new monkey wrench.
   C) Johnson was the greatest fighter ever.
   D) Tommy Burns fought Johnson in 1908.

WRITE ABOUT—

6. Jack Johnson, the first African-American heavyweight champ, was the victim of prejudice. So was Jackie Robinson, the first African-American in major league baseball. Was there any difference in the way the two men reacted to this prejudice? If so, what was it?

17
THE BOAT PEOPLE
FROM VIETNAM

In 1975, the Vietnam War ended. Communists from the North ruled the whole of Vietnam. Many South Vietnamese wanted to leave their country. Many of them wanted to come to America some day. But the only way to escape from Vietnam was by boat.

The only Vietnamese boats were small fishing boats. Fishermen only went a few miles. They fished near the shore. Their boats were not made to cross the open sea. Any trip in these boats was risky and dangerous. Their wooden planks were rotting. Many boats had holes. But the Vietnamese were desperate. They tried to escape by boat anyway. They became known as the boat people.

Many boats sank. If the people in the boats were lucky, a passing ship saved them. If not, they drowned. More than 150,000 Vietnamese boat people drowned between 1975 and 1979.

Pirates were a terrible danger. They thought the boat people had money and jewelry. So the seas around Vietnam filled up with pirate boats. Some pirates robbed, but gave food and water in return. Others hurt or killed the people in the boats.

One boat was attacked by twenty pirates. They were armed with guns and hammers. They demanded gold, money and other valuables. They searched the boat to make sure nothing was hidden. Before they left, they removed the boat engine. For seven days and nights, the boat drifted on the open ocean. Finally, it landed several hundred miles away, in the country of Malaysia.

A 22-year-old woman was on one of these boats. She said all the passengers were squeezed together. They had no food. The only water was rain water. They caught it in cups to have something to drink. There was no shade from the sun. When a storm came, they almost drowned. She got sick and threw up a lot. She looked and smelled terrible. That was lucky for her. When pirates attacked the boat, she was left alone.

Another Vietnamese girl had a similar story. She and her mother climbed aboard a 19-foot boat. More people climbed on. And still more. There was no space left. They were squashed together. The boat was built to hold 30 people. When it left, it carried 465 passengers! Some men hung onto the side of the boat. People tied bags of rice on their bodies. This was their food for the journey. The boat set out across the open seas.

The boats bounced on the waves. Many people got seasick. Each day was the same. The children cried. People tried to find a comfortable position. And always more ocean. This boat was also attacked by pirates. This was very dangerous for young women. The girl who told the story was lucky. She hid behind some bundles. The pirates didn't find her. Finally, the boat reached Malaysia.

Trouble was not over for these boat people. When they landed in a foreign country, they were taken to special camps. Everything in a camp cost money. They had to pay for their food and the huts they lived in. One girl was lucky. She had a gold chain. She cut it into small bits and used the pieces to buy food. She could not eat much. For two years, her gold chain was all the money she had.

Some of the boat people finally came to America. Life was still hard. Many Americans welcomed them, but others didn't want them around. The Vietnamese had to deal with these people. They had to learn English. They had to find jobs. But they were glad to be alive. The terrible boat trip was over.

GLOSSARY

desperate Willing to take dangerous chances because of despair.

pirates Sea robbers.

EXERCISES

REFERENCE

1. If you wanted to see how far it is from Vietnam to Malaysia, what would you use?

   A) an atlas
   B) a dictionary
   C) an encyclopedia
   D) an almanac

CAUSE/EFFECT

2. Why did pirates attack the boat people?

   A) The boat people attacked them first.
   B) They didn't like Vietnamese people.
   C) They were working for the Communists.
   D) They believed the boat people had lots of money.

MAKING JUDGMENTS

3. Why did so many boat people drown?

   A) Pirates threw them overboard.
   B) They killed themselves.
   C) The boats were rotten and many sank.
   D) The boats hit underwater rocks.

VOCABULARY DEVELOPMENT

4. A young nurse described <u>what happened</u> on one of the boats. Which words have the same meaning as "what happened"?

   A) her unhappiness
   B) her experiences
   C) her life story
   D) her dreams

OUTLINING

5. What belongs in the missing part of this outline?

    I)   People left Vietnam in small boats.
    II) Many boats were attacked by pirates.
    III) ....
    IV) Some Vietnamese got jobs in America.

    A) The Vietnam war ended.
    B) Communists ruled the whole of Vietnam.
    C) Many people got on a small boat.
    D) Some of the boats finally reached land.

FACT/OPINION

6. Which statement contains an <u>opinion</u>?

    A) The pirates took money and jewelry.
    B) The Communists were bad rulers.
    C) Some boats had holes.
    D) Many people drowned.

WRITE ABOUT—

7. Make a list of at least 5 things that might make people try to escape from their country, the way the people in the story did.

18
REVIEW QUESTIONS

I. CROSSWORD

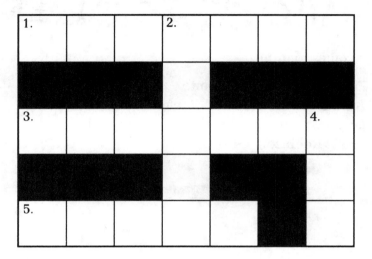

CLUES ACROSS

1. Jackie Robinson's team.
3. They terrified the Boat People.
5. Jack Johnson was a great ___.

CLUES DOWN

2. Small, soft fruit picked by Panchito
4. And this was all the Boat People saw all day.

II. WHAT HAPPENS TWICE?

6. You have read two stories about Panchito and his family. One event occurs in both stories. Which one?

A) Panchito got a trumpet.
B) The family moved into Mr. Sullivan's garage.
C) The family packed everything into cardboard boxes.
D) Mama carried her cooking pot with great care.

III. WHAT'S IN THE PICTURE?

Who comes to mind?

A) Panchito's brother, Roberto
B) A pirate in the seas off Vietnam
C) Jack Johnson
D) Jackie Robinson

72

19
THE TOUGH HANDS OF NANCY LOPEZ

In 1960, golf was a sport that Anglos played. It was very hard for a Mexican-American to become a professional golfer. It was harder still if that Mexican-American was a woman. Then along came Nancy Lopez. She did the impossible. Nancy, a Mexican-American woman, became a champion golfer. How did she do it?

Nancy got started in golf when she was a small child. Her father liked to play. Young Nancy often went with him to the golf course. One day, Mr. Lopez let Nancy play. She hit the ball long and hard. It headed straight for the hole. She did it several times more. Her father realized Nancy could be a great golfer.

Nancy practiced and practiced. The skin on her hands became really hard. Golfers' hands need this tough skin. At home, she never had to wash the dishes. Water might soften her skin. Do you think Nancy was upset that she couldn't wash dishes?

Nancy joined the golf team in high school. She was the only girl on the team. The boys liked playing with her. She hit the ball as far as the boys did. The boys on the other teams didn't like Nancy so much, however. She could beat them. They didn't like losing to a girl.

When she got out of school, Nancy became a professional golfer. She was a success right away. In her first year, she was named Rookie of the Year. She won a lot of tournaments. Soon she was making big money.

People like Nancy. She's very human. She lets people know how things are going with her. She used to be rather chubby. She ate lots of fattening foods. One day she went on a strict diet. She ate nothing between meals except apples and raisins. Slowly she lost weight. Nancy was very pleased, and so were her many fans.

In 1982, Nancy married Ray Knight, a baseball player. Nancy and Ray had the same problems as other two-career couples. Nancy wanted to keep playing golf. Ray wanted to stay in baseball. This meant they had to spend many weeks apart. Nancy wasn't happy about the problem, but she didn't let it hurt her golf. One year, she won five tournaments and was named top Woman Athlete of the Year!

PHOTOFEST

Mexican-American Golf Champion Nancy Lopez lines up her putt on her way to another golf championship.

GLOSSARY

chubby   Plump.

professional golfer   Someone who plays golf for a living.

tournaments   Athletic contests where many players play each other to find which one is the best.

EXERCISES

SENTENCE COMPLETION

1. The year Nancy turned professional, she was named _____.

   A) Golfer of the Year
   B) Rookie of the Year
   C) Top Woman Athlete of the Year
   D) Winner of Five Tournaments

SEQUENCE

2. What happened first?

   A) Nancy married Ray Knight.
   B) Nancy stopped washing the dishes.
   C) Nancy started to make big money playing golf.
   D) Nancy's father started Nancy playing golf.

MAKING JUDGMENTS

3. Which is true?

   A) In 1960, most golfers were Mexican-Americans.
   B) Nancy hated golf at first.
   C) Most professional golfers are men.
   D) Most Mexican Americans are good golfers.

MAKING JUDGMENTS

4. From the selection, which of the following seems to be a problem for Nancy?
   A) a bad temper
   B) a tendency to overweight
   C) an unwillingness to practice
   D) a weak drive

WRITE ABOUT—

5. Suppose you could be a professional athlete. What kind of athlete would you be, and why?

20
ENRIQUE'S REVOLT

Bartolomé de las Casas was a young Spanish soldier at the time of Columbus. He helped conquer the island of Cuba and was given a large amount of land as a reward. He could have become very rich. But then he saw how Spanish landowners used the Tainos and other Native Americans of Cuba as slaves. Thousands of these Indians died.

Las Casas hated what he saw. He became a priest. He spent the rest of his life trying to protect Native Americans.

To tell the world what was happening, Las Casas wrote a book called *History of the Indies*. Here is a part of that book. It is the true story of an Indian chief whom the Spanish called Enrique. Enrique lived on the island of Hispaniola in what is now the country of Santo Domingo. For fourteen years he fought against the Spanish. In particular, he fought against a Spanish soldier named Valenzuela.

From here on, Las Casas tells the story:

Like all Spaniards, Valenzuela thought of Enrique as a slave. He called him a dog and all sorts of rude names. He attacked Enrique's men. But they fought back. They fought so fiercely they killed two or three Spaniards and wounded many more. The rest were forced to retreat. But Enrique refused to follow the fleeing Spaniards. He said, "Be thankful, Valenzuela, that I spare your life. Go away and never come back."

Valenzuela and his men ran. They hurried back to San Juan de la Maguana. Valenzuela's pride was badly hurt. News of Enrique's rebellion spread all over the island. The Governor soon learned of it. He ordered that Enrique must be stopped. Seventy or eighty soldiers went to hunt him down. They could not find him. They grew tired and hungry as they searched. Finally, they tracked him down in the mountains. But truly, the soldiers were the ones who were hunted down. For when they met, it was the soldiers who lost the fight. Some were killed, others were wounded. Those who survived fled. This badly hurt their pride.

Enrique became famous all over the island. Three hundred Indians left their homes and went to join him. They called him their chief. He taught them how to defend themselves. He insisted that his men must never attack the enemy first.

Enrique's Indians were very tough. They could fight hand to hand with the Spanish soldiers for a whole day. They armed themselves with Spanish weapons. Some Indians seized their weapons from the soldiers. Others took their masters' weapons and then joined Enrique.

Enrique was very careful about the safety of his men. He worked out all the places where the soldiers might attack. Then he put spies and guards there. When these spies told him the Spanish were close by, Enrique acted quickly. He and fifty warriors took all the women, children, and old men to mountain hideouts. These secret places had plenty of food.

He left behind his young nephew, who was three feet tall. This young man was very short and very brave. He and the other Indians fought the attacking Spaniards like lions. Finally Enrique returned with fresh troops. He attacked the Spanish army at a weak point. The Spanish lost many men that time.

Many times the soldiers attacked Enrique. And every time, Enrique made them turn tail. The defeated army ran away. One time, 72 Spaniards were fleeing. They hid in a cave from the Indians following them. The Indians wanted to start a fire. But Enrique stopped them. He said, "I do not want them burned; take away their weapons and let them go." On this occasion, the Indians seized many fine swords. They had to learn how to use them.

One of these Spanish soldiers later became a monk. He had promised to do this if he escaped from the cave alive. It shows what a good man Enrique was. He could easily have killed every single soldier that day.

After reporting these exciting events, Las Casas tells us no more about Enrique. Perhaps he died leading his men in battle. Perhaps he died of smallpox, a disease brought to America by the Europeans. But his revolt was not forgotten. He was one of America's first freedom fighters.

GLOSSARY

hand to hand   Very close—close enough to use weapons like swords and clubs.

warriors   Fighters or soldiers.

monk   A man who withdraws from everyday life and devotes his life to religion.

EXERCISES

MAIN IDEA

1. Who was Enrique?

    A) a Spanish general
    B) an Indian priest
    C) a fighting Indian
    D) a Spanish priest

VOCABULARY DEVELOPMENT

2. Paragraph 2 of the selection tells how Spanish soldiers found Enrique in the mountains. Which word or words in the selection have the same meaning as <u>found</u>?

    A) learned
    B) tracked down
    C) searched
    D) survived

DRAWING CONCLUSIONS

3. Enrique spared Valenzuela's life.

    Enrique would not let the Spanish soldiers be burned.

    Las Casas uses these two facts to show that Enrique was—

    A) a great general.
    B) a brave fighter.
    C) a short man.
    D) a good man.

MAIN IDEA

4. The main idea if this selection is that—

    A) Enrique was a poor leader.
    B) Valenzuela hated Enrique.
    C) Enrique led a long, successful revolt.
    D) The Indians had many Spanish weapons.

IDIOM

5. Las Casas tells us that Enrique made the Spaniards <u>turn tail</u>. Someone who "turns tail"—

   A) runs away.
   B) fights hard.
   C) comes last.
   D) spins around and around.

COMPARE/ CONTRAST

6. How was Las Casas different from other Spanish landowners?

   A) He was an enemy of the Church.
   B) He was the brother of the King of Spain.
   C) He wouldn't treat the Indians badly.
   D) He was far richer than anyone else.

WRITE ABOUT—

7. Selection 3 told you about a Native American named Guarionex. He lived on the same island that Enrique did, at about the same time.

   Write a few sentences telling what is similar and what is different about these two men and their lives.

21
TALKING WITH DIEGO AND FRIDA

Here is an imaginary talk between two people. Diego Rivera and Frida Kahlo are speaking.

DIEGO: Well, Frida, what can we tell these people about ourselves?

FRIDA: Tell them what we look like.

DIEGO: My wife, Frida, is a real Mexican beauty. She's quite tiny. She has long, black hair. Sometimes she pins it up and sticks flowers in it.

Oh—Most people have two eyebrows. Frida only has one. Her eyebrows meet in the middle.

FRIDA: And you're a big bear. You're so fat, you can't find a shop with clothes your size.

DIEGO: Come on, Frida. You know you like my rolls of fat.

FRIDA: He's so vain. Let's tell them how we earn a living. We paint. Diego paints very big paintings. He paints them on the walls of buildings. They're called murals. They're all over Mexico City. You see them everywhere. They're gigantic, and very exciting to look at. Many of them show events from Mexico's history. I'm very proud of my husband. He's a great painter.

DIEGO: Tell them about your own work, Frida.

FRIDA: Well, my work isn't as important as Diego's.

DIEGO: Nonsense, Frida. People love your work. You were the first Mexican to have a painting in the Louvre.

FRIDA: That's the main art museum in Paris. Just in case you don't know, friends.

DIEGO: You were the first Latino painter to make big bucks in New York. One of your paintings sold for 1.5 million dollars.

FRIDA: OK, OK. It's true some people like my work. But I don't paint big murals like Diego. My paintings are small. They can hang on the wall. They're about me. When I paint I have a mirror in front of me. I need to know exactly how I look. Sometimes I put Diego in my paintings, too.

DIEGO: Yes. In strange places, too. Frida paints her head and shoulders. Then, right above her nose, she paints my face.

FRIDA: Yes, stupido. You're on my mind all the time. But tell them what you paint, Diego.

DIEGO: Maybe they won't be happy when I tell them. I'm not like most Americans. I'm a communist. I paint like a communist.

FRIDA: Yes. My husband wants to get rid of the millionaires. He wants us all to be equal. Here in Mexico, he wants us all to be equally poor. Seriously, Diego is a great fan of Russia.

DIEGO: Yes. I admire Lenin. He used to be Russia's leader. I put him in a lot of paintings.

FRIDA: You tried to put Lenin's face in your great New York mural. But that didn't work out.

DIEGO: They were fools! It was that millionaire, Nelson Rockefeller. He asked me to paint the wall of the RCA building. Of course I put the great communist Lenin in the picture. Rockefeller didn't like that.

FRIDA: No surprise, Diego. A millionaire doesn't want to pay for a picture of a communist.

DIEGO: I had almost finished. The wall was almost all painted. They made me stop working. Then they chipped my painting off the wall and threw it away.

FRIDA: Diego and I are Mexico's most famous painters. I died still young. I was in pain most of my life. A lot of my pain came from you, Diego. You were a no-good husband. But we had a lot of fun too, didn't we Diego? Look out for our work.

GLOSSARY

vain   Too proud of one's looks.

EXERCISES

WHO IS SPEAKING?

1. Who is speaking?

   "I paint murals. I like to include communist leaders in my murals."

   A) Frida Kahlo
   B) Diego Rivera

WHO IS SPEAKING

2. Who is speaking?

   "I'm very fat. No stores carries clothes my size."

   A) Frida Kahlo
   B) Diego Rivera

WHO IS SPEAKING

3. Who is speaking?

   "When I paint I have a mirror in front of me. I need to know exactly how I look."

   A) Frida Kahlo
   B) Diego Rivera

DRAWING CONCLUSIONS

4. Where would you be most likely to see a mural?

   A) on a wall
   B) on the ground
   C) on an easel
   D) in the sky

MAKING JUDGMENTS

5. Why was Diego's painting removed from the RCA building?

    A) It was a bad painting.
    B) It was being taken to a museum.
    C) Rockefeller didn't like communists.
    D) Lenin didn't want to be in the painting.

FIGURATIVE LANGUAGE

6. Frida says Diego is on her mind all the time. What does it mean to say someone is "on your mind"?

    A) Someone is pressing against your head.
    B) You are angry with someone.
    C) You have a message for someone.
    D) You can't stop thinking about someone.

REFERENCE

7. Where would you look for Frida's paintings?

    A) On walls in Mexico City
    B) In an art museum
    C) In a theater
    D) In the RCA building

CHARACTERS' VIEWPOINT

8. How do you think Frida and Diego feel about each other's paintings?

    A) ashamed
    B) proud
    C) critical
    D) jealous

WRITE ABOUT

9. Suppose you were a painter. What kind of paintings would you like to paint? Why do you want to paint this way?

22
THE INDIANS WHO WERE NEVER DEFEATED

In the early 1800's Alabama was the home of the Creek Indians. At that time, the Creeks' rights to their lands were in danger. White people were moving into Alabama. They were settling on land that belonged to the Creeks.

One day, a visitor came from far-off Indiana. He was the great chief Tecumseh, leader of another Indian nation. He told the Creeks that the white men were grabbing Indian lands all over the country. All the tribes must join together and fight. The Creeks listened carefully to Tecumseh. Many of them decided he was right. They must fight!

In 1814 the Creeks attacked. They killed hundreds of white settlers. But the settlers raised an army. Led by General Andrew Jackson, the soldiers met the Indians at the battle of Horseshoe Bend. The Creeks fought hard, but Jackson won. The Creeks were beaten.

Many of the Creeks fled south to Florida. There they joined their relatives, the Seminole Indians. Among the Creeks who fled was a 10-year-old boy who was later given the name Osceola.

The Creeks and Seminoles thought they were safe in Florida. At that time Florida was not part of the United States. It was owned by Spain. But when Osceola was 18, Florida was taken over by the United States. Its first governor was the Indians' old enemy, General Andrew Jackson. Jackson wanted all Indians to leave. If they left, white men could take over all of Florida. There was a short, bitter war. When it was over, most of the Seminoles were forced onto a reservation. Osceola, who had become a young war leader, was among them.

By 1829, Andrew Jackson was President of the United States. In 1834 he tried again to force the Seminoles to leave Florida. He sent a letter to the Seminole chiefs on the reservation. If they signed it, they would be paid to leave Florida and settle far in the West. Several chiefs signed. Osceola refused. Furiously, he drew his hunting knife and stabbed it down through the paper.

For nearly two months Osceola led the resistance to signing President Jackson's paper. Finally, some soldiers grabbed him. They chained him up in jail. To get out, he agreed to sign.

But soon he started fighting again. He led some of his people out of the reservation. They hid in the Florida swamps. Hundreds of other Seminoles joined Osceola. Whole villages left their farms. In the swamps, they were safe. From time to time, bands of Seminole warriors came out of hiding. They attacked white settlers and white soldiers. Then they hid in the swamps again.

Among the fiercest of the Seminole fighters were African-Americans. For many years, African-Americans had found safety with the Seminoles. They were men and women who escaped from slavery. Many of them married into the Seminole tribe. Osceola's own wife was the child of a black woman. If the Indians surrendered, these free people and their children would be slaves again.

Over and over Osceola and the Seminoles beat the soldiers. But President Jackson sent thousands more soldiers against Osceola. Some of the Seminoles surrendered and moved West. But not Osceola. He said, "We will fight until the last drop of our blood sinks into these lands of ours."

For two years Osceola's people fought. Once, Osceola agreed to give up. But then he learned that white slave catchers were being allowed to round up black and part-black Seminoles as slaves. He disappeared back into the swamps, and the war went on.

In 1837, Osceola asked for another meeting. He was ill and tired of fighting. He said his people were willing to make peace, but they would not leave their homeland. The white soldiers seized him. The meeting was just a trick. Osceola was sent to an island where he could not escape. There, a few months later, he died.

Deep in the swamps, the rest of the Seminoles fought on. Finally, the United States gave up trying to beat them. Today, the great-grandchildren of the fighting Seminoles live peacefully in Florida. They never signed a treaty. They never sold their lands. They were never defeated, and they never surrendered. Osceola would be proud.

GLOSSARY

furiously Angrily.

swamps Wetlands covered with trees.

warriors Fighters in a war.

OSCEOLA

Osceola, the leader of the fighting Seminole Indians of Florida. He was never defeated and never surrendered. Captured by a trick, he died only a few days after this portrait was painted.

EXERCISES

OUTLINING

1. What belongs in the missing part of this outline?

   I)   The Creeks were defeated.
   II) Osceola refused to give up the Seminole lands.
   III) ....
   IV)   Osceola was tricked.
   V)   The Seminoles survive.

   A) Osceola moved to Florida.
   B) Osceola and the Seminoles fled to the swamps.
   C) Osceola was imprisoned.
   D) Jackson became President

SYNONYMS

2. The author says <u>bands</u> of Seminole warriors attacked the soldiers. Which word means the same as "bands?"

   A) groups
   B) rings
   C) houses
   D) millions

MAKING JUDGMENTS

3. Why did Andrew Jackson want the Seminoles to leave Florida?

   A) He wanted the Creek Indians to live there.
   B) He thought they would like to live in the West.
   C) He wanted white men to have their lands.
   D) He was afraid they would get sick.

AUTHOR'S VIEWPOINT

4. What does the author probably think of Osceola?

    A) He took too many risks.
    B) He didn't know when to give up.
    C) He was a fool to let people cheat him.
    D) He was a good leader.

FACT/ OPINION

5. Which statement contains an <u>opinion</u>?

    A) The Seminoles never signed a treaty.
    B) Ex-slaves lived in the swamps
    C) Osceola was very brave.
    D) Andrew Jackson was Governor of Florida.

VOCABULARY DEVELOPMENT

6. Many Seminoles were <u>caught</u> and killed. Which word has the same meaning as "caught"?

    A) insulted
    B) helped
    C) tricked
    D) captured

WRITE ABOUT—

7. Imagine that you are the leader of a band of Seminole Indians. You and the people in your band are discussing whether to leave Florida and go West or whether to stay and fight. What is your advice, and what are your reasons for it?

23
THE ONE AND ONLY ROBERTO CLEMENTE

To play pro baseball, you have to be good. Some players are very good. But Roberto Clemente was great. He was one of the greatest baseball stars of all time.

Roberto was born in Puerto Rico in 1934. His father was the foreman of a sugar plantation. The family lived in a fine house. Home was a good place. There was lots of love and affection.

Roberto played in his first baseball game when he was eight. He played on a team with his older brothers. Roberto was good at many sports: the 400 meter run, the javelin throw, the high jump. But he wasn't too interested in them. The sport that really mattered was baseball. Roberto remembered how he forgot to come home and eat. All he wanted to do was play baseball. Sometimes he played for ten, twelve hours a day.

In 1952, Roberto began to play for money. He joined the Puerto Rican Winter League. His pay was $40 a week. The League had some fine players. Some of the great African-American players played there. Puerto Rican baseball had no color bar.

One of Roberto's teammates was a young man named Willie Mays, who later became another of baseball's really great players. Willie coached Roberto and showed him the finer points of the game. Willie was Roberto's idol. But Roberto always said he didn't play like Willie. His style was his own. He played like Roberto Clemente.

Roberto was strong. He was nearly six feet tall. He weighed around 180 pounds. His features were fine, and his skin was very dark. He was good-looking. Most remarkable were his hands. They were huge. Someone said he looked as though he was always wearing baseball gloves.

Roberto could make amazing catches. He could catch the ball as he banged into a wall. He caught balls while sliding on his belly or on his shoulder. You need strong arms to throw the ball a long way. Roberto had them. He could throw out a runner hundreds of feet away. His batting was spectacular too. Most hitters have one weakness at least. Some can't hit curve balls. Some can't hit inside pitches. Clemente could hit anything. One of baseball's greatest pitchers was asked the best way to pitch to Clemente. He replied, "Try rolling the ball along the ground."

GLOSSARY

foreman The boss of a group of workers.

plantation A large farm.

javelin A kind of spear.

color bar A custom that doesn't allow a black person to play on a team.

inside pitches Pitches that come close to the batter's body ("Inside" home plate).

discrimination Laws and customs against blacks, Asians, Latinos, etc.

malaria A serious disease of the blood.

insomnia Sleeplessness.

tendons The stringy part of a muscle that attaches the muscle to a bone.

Many teams wanted to hire Roberto. He signed with the Brooklyn Dodgers in 1954. The next year, he transferred to the Pittsburgh Pirates. The Pirates were in trouble at the time. They were usually at the bottom of the National League. Once they signed Clemente, things picked up. In 1960, they won the National League pennant.

In 1964, Clemente married Vera Zabala. They had three sons. Someone joked that Roberto and Vera produced a whole outfield.

But life wasn't easy for a Puerto Rican, even one as talented as Roberto Clemente. His English was still poor. His black skin meant that he suffered discrimination. He was treated like the African-American players. Many hotels and restaurants refused to serve him. He could not eat with his teammates. Sports writers made fun of his poor English. This angered Roberto. Also, he thought—and he was probably right—that some umpires were prejudiced against anyone with a black skin.

Then there were the injuries. Roberto suffered from malaria. He had loose bone chips in his elbow. His spine was curved. He also had loose spinal discs, swollen thighs, insomnia, headaches, nervous stomach, pulled muscles, and strained tendons. Roberto talked a lot about his problems. His teammates teased him. "Oh, how I hurt, hurt," he would moan. But everyone knew that the worse Clemente felt, the better he played.

In 1966, he was voted the National League's Most Valuable Player. Then came 1971. This was Roberto's year of miracles. All year long, he played superbly. Pittsburgh got into the World Series. *Time* Magazine said he won the Series all by himself.

Clemente became a national hero in Puerto Rico—partly because of baseball, partly because he spoke up for Latinos. During the off-season, he traveled round North and South America. He spoke for his people. He was extraordinarily generous. He loaned out money and never bothered about getting it back. He adored children. He gave hundreds of signed baseballs to his small fans. He would always stop and chat with an admirer. He gave money to buy legs for an injured child. His home in San Juan was always filled with charity meetings. He planned to build sports camps for boys and girls all over Puerto Rico.

These plans came to an end on New Year's Eve, 1972. An earthquake in Nicaragua had killed 6,000 people and injured 20,000 more. Clemente led a Puerto Rican relief effort. On December 31, he climbed aboard an old plane filled with supplies for the earthquake victims. The plane crashed into the sea. Roberto's body was never recovered. All Puerto Rico mourned his death.

Almost immediately, Roberto was nominated for Baseball's Hall of Fame. Usually a player must wait for five years before he is elected. But for Roberto, the rule was ignored. On March 20, Roberto Clemente became the first Latino ballplayer to be elected to the Hall of Fame.

EXERCISES

VOCABULARY DEVELOPMENT

1. Roberto Clemente was an extremely powerful hitter. His batting was <u>extraordinary</u>. Which word has the same meaning as "extraordinary?"

   A) strange
   B) slow
   C) smooth
   D) spectacular

FIGURATIVE LANGUAGE

2. The selection says that Vera Clemente <u>produced a whole outfield</u>. This means that she—

   A) trained the outfield for Roberto's team.
   B) sowed new grass in the outfield.
   C) had nine children, one for each position on a baseball team.
   D) had three children, one for each outfield position.

SEQUENCE

3. Which came <u>last</u>?

    A) Nicaragua had an earthquake .
    B) Roberto married Vera.
    C) Roberto signed with the Pirates.
    D) Pittsburgh won the World Series.

CAUSE/EFFECT

4. Roberto had many injuries and sicknesses. According to the selection, how did they affect his playing?

    A) They slowed him down a lot.
    B) The worse he felt, the better he played.
    C) His injuries and sicknesses weren't real at all.
    D) His sicknesses forced him to retire from baseball.

REFERENCE

5. If you wanted to know who won the World Series in 1990, you would use—

    A) a dictionary
    B) an almanac
    C) an atlas
    D) a thesaurus

VOCABULARY DEVELOPMENT

6. Roberto Clemente was treated badly because of his skin color. He was <u>treated differently</u> from white players. Which words have the same meaning as "treated differently"?

    A) suffered from
    B) discriminated against
    C) played badly
    D) held up

WRITE ABOUT—

7. In how many different ways was Roberto Clemente a hero? Which do you think he would he have valued the most?

24
REVIEW QUESTIONS

I. WHO IS SPEAKING?

1. "We don't want the white man's money."

   "My great-great-great-granddaughter still lives in Florida."

   "Quick! Hurry! Back to the swamps."

   A) Osceola
   B) Enrique
   C) Diego Rivera
   D) Roberto Clemente

2. "Oh! Oh! How I hurt."

   "I was great at everything—running, hitting, and fielding."

   "I died in a plane crash."

   A) Osceola
   B) Roberto Clemente
   C) Nancy Lopez
   D) Frida Kahlo

3. "Be thankful that I spare your life."

   "Never, never attack the enemy first."

   "Nephew, I leave you in command. Fight bravely."

   A) Diego Rivera
   B) Osceola
   C) Enrique
   D) Valenzuela

4. "I'm not allowed to wash dishes. I'm not sorry."

   "Maybe I could eat just one more Tootsie Roll."

   "Of course I miss my husband, but I must play."

   A) Frida Kahlo
   B) Osceola
   C) Enrique's wife
   D) Nancy Lopez

II. MISSING PERSONS

In each of these passages a person's name is hidden. The passage also gives a clue about the hidden person. Draw a line under the letters of the name in each sentence.

5. Uncle! Me 'n Terry want to go watch the baseball game.

6. I know an Indian named Henri. Question—where does he live? Answer—in Hispaniola.

7. I won't change what I paint. I'd rather die. God save me from millionaires who tell me what to paint.

8. Put the golf ball in an envelope. Zip it up. Send it to a fan.

III. WHO IS IT?

Some people are famous for something about the way they look. Match the body part with its owner.

9. One eyebrow

   A) Panchito
   B) Frida Kahlo
   C) Nancy Lopez
   D) Jack Johnson

10. A face without scars

   A) Frida Kahlo
   B) Roberto Clemente
   C) Jack Johnson
   D) Jackie Robinson

11. Huge hands

    A) Roberto Clemente
    B) Frida Kahlo
    C) Nancy Lopez
    D) Diego Rivera

12. Only three feet tall

    A) Jack Johnson
    B) Enrique's nephew
    C) Osceola's fighters
    D) Panchito's mother

IV. WHO WAS FIRST?

13. First African-American to play in baseball's Major Leagues.

    A) Roberto Clemente
    B) Jackie Robinson

14. First Mexican artist to have a painting in Paris' Louvre Museum.
    A) Frida Kahlo
    B) Diego Rivera

15. First freedom fighters.

    A) Enrique and his Tainos
    B) Osceola and the Seminoles

16. First woman of Mexican ancestry to be named Woman Athlete of the Year.

    A) Frida Kahlo
    B) Nancy Lopez

V. WRITE ABOUT

17. This book has told the stories of many heroic people. Which one do you admire most, and why?